2-10-2000

To Sarah
Lee

Love always,

Grandma & Grandpa
Lupinski

Presented to

On

From

Friend Jesus

Prayers for Children

GAYNELL BORDES CRONIN

ST. ANTHONY MESSENGER PRESS

Cincinnati, Ohio

Dedication

For those little ones, my own
    grandchildren—
Sarah, Maggie, Peter, Emma, Tess
    and Luke—
who show me the face of God daily
    and renew me in the simplicity
    and love of prayer in my own life,

I thank you

Nihil Obstat: Rev. Nicholas Lohkamp, O.F.M.
            Rev. Robert J. Hagedorn
Imprimi Potest: Rev. John Bok, O.F.M.
            Provincial
Imprimatur: +Most Rev. Carl K. Moeddel, V.G.
            Archdiocese of Cincinnati
            April 26, 1999

The *nihil obstat* and *imprimatur* are a declaration that a book
is considered to be free from doctrinal or moral error. It is
not implied that those who have granted the *nihil obstat* and
imprimatur agree with the contents, opinions or statements
expressed.

Cover and interior illustrations by Chris Sickels
Cover and book design by Constance Wolfer

ISBN 0-86716-360-7

Published by St. Anthony Messenger Press
Printed in the U.S.A.

Contents

PRAYERS FOR OTHERS

PRAYERS FOR THE WEEK

May Jesus Be Your Friend

When I was a child, I lived in the South, and we called dragonflies "mosquito hawks." I spent hours watching them. I never disturbed these colorful insects because I was afraid they might land on me. But I learned a great lesson watching mosquito hawks: If you sit still, your mind stops "hopping" from one thing to another and your restless body learns to stay in the moment.

I invite you to sit quietly and find a place to welcome God into your own heart. "I am with you always," our friend Jesus tells us. We can find Jesus when we watch mosquito hawks and also when we have problems getting along with others, when we don't do what we should do, when we are most happy and when we are most sad. This book offers you a way to pray about the things that happen to you every day at home, at school, when you are alone and when you are with others.

We pray to love someone, not to get anything, and to become the person God is calling us to be, not all at once, but step by step. Wherever we turn, we find the face of God. May you grow in love with God and God's people. May Jesus always be your friend.

— *Gaynell Bordes Cronin*

PART ONE

Prayers for Me

"I call you my friends."
John 15:15

TIME OUT CORNER

When I Just Don't Fit

Some days, friend Jesus,
I JUST DON'T FIT.

Other kids tease me.
They make fun of my weight.
They ignore me. They laugh at me.
I JUST DON'T FIT.

They whisper behind my back.
They won't let me into their group.
I JUST DON'T FIT.

Some kids are smart
      and others make jokes about them.
Some kids have trouble in school
      and others make fun of them.
I JUST DON'T FIT.

My favorite pants don't fit anymore.
I've grown and my shoes don't fit.

Help me to remember that
      in your love, Jesus,
      I fit.

I always have and I always will.

Trouble With Friends

Friend Jesus,
last year, school was simple.
It was easy to get along with friends.

What happened? Life is so tough now.

People say,
"Whose friend are you?"
    OR
"Go away. You can't play with my friend."
    OR
"If you are her friend, you can't be my friend."

Did you ever have trouble
with your friends, Jesus?

What should I do?

Walk with me and
    be my friend, Jesus,
    as I learn about
    being a friend.

Love

Friend Jesus,
    you call us to love and be loved.

Help me name all the people who love me:

    ____.

Now, be with me as I name all the people I love:

    ____.

Thank you, friend Jesus, for loving us and
    showing us how to love.

Not Yet

I want to forgive my friend for not letting me into the group to play,

> but NOT YET.

I want to tell my Mom the truth about what happened in school,

> but NOT YET.

I want to let my brother know I don't like being picked on,

> but NOT YET.

I am afraid if I pray, God, you will convince me to change and forgive,

> but I can't do that—
>
> NOT YET.

In Trouble

I'm in big trouble, God.

I did something I wasn't supposed to do
   and now ____ is upset with me.

When I misbehave, I feel ____.
   I was wrong. I didn't listen.

Rules are made to protect and help others.
   I'm sorry.

I need your help, God,
   to find the words
   to talk about this trouble with someone.

   Please.

Homework

TV. Cartoons. Video games. Computer.
Phone calls. Cards. A ball game outside.
Friends knocking at my door.

It is easy to get distracted
    when there is homework to do.

I work at school all day. I'm tired.
    I need a break.
Really, I'm pretty good at making excuses
and avoiding homework.
    But homework is important.

Did you ever have homework, Jesus?
Maybe we can do this together.

Help me to set aside time for homework,
to get my things together that I need and
    then to do my homework!

When I am finished, **then** I will play.

Play Date

When friends come to my house, I say,
    "welcome," "come in."
I'm glad to see them. I'm happy to spend
    time with them.

Did you have friends over, Jesus?

We call these times play dates.
You set a time and a place to meet.
    You play together.
You get to know one another.

And when you say good-bye,
    you promise to get together again.

I'd like to make a play date with you, Jesus,
    on _____ at _____.

Say No

God of Courage,
sometimes
    I need to say NO,
    I ought to say NO,
    I want to say NO,
    but I am afraid.

I need courage to say NO to friends
    when they ask me to do things
    that I know are wrong and
    could hurt others.

I need help to say NO to myself
    when I begin to tease,
    make fun of someone
    or say "Go away, you can't play with us."

God of Courage,
    give me strength to say NO.

Everything Goes Wrong Day

Friend Jesus,
   what a day!

Everything seemed to go wrong at home,
   at school, at play.

Maybe it was me, maybe it was others,
   maybe it was something said or done.

It could have been ____,
   but I'm not sure.

I'm feeling very little,
   and people seem to hurt me easily.

Whew! I'm glad this day is over.
   Be with me as I sleep.

And then, YES, tomorrow,
   Let's begin a new day together.

Time

Morning, noon, night.
All time is for you, God.

Feeling Sad

Friend Jesus,
I know that sometimes you were sad.
   Me, too.

My face changes when I am sad.
My eyes and mouth feel droopy, and
   nothing in me feels like moving.

Sit with me in my sadness, Jesus.
   Let me not run away.

I am sad now because ____.

Thank you, Jesus, for being with me.
   With you I am never alone.

Hands

God of Helping Hands,
    use my hands
    to bring peace and joy
    to those I meet today
      and every day.

Feet

With my feet I walk and run, hop, skip, jump.

Feet, where did you go today? To the
    beach
        playground
           store
               school
                  friend's house
                     Grandma's?

Today, my feet took me to ____.

On my feet I wear shoes, sandals, sneakers, slippers.
    My favorite shoes are ____.

Help me, wherever I go, God,
    to walk gently on your earth
      which hears my every sound and
        feels my every step.

After a Fight With a Friend

Most days, I like my friends.

But, sometimes, well, sometimes,
I get so mad at them when
    they wreck my game,
    or call me names, or
    won't let me play with them.

It is hard to like them when they are mean to me.

Let me remember how much
    you always love me, God,
    and love them, too.

Help me to be like you—
    loving, caring, forgiving my friends.

Today, I want to thank you
    for my friend, ____.

Moving

Moving to a new place to live,
    to a new school and new friends —
    it is not easy, Jesus.

Give me courage to say good-bye.
    Make me brave. Help me discover
    a new world of fun and friends.

Give me courage to say hello.

Bless the newness of house, school, people.

God of Love

May I see you in every face.
May I hear you in every voice.
May I welcome you in every person I meet.

Sports

God of Playgrounds and Fields,
    running and kicking the ball in soccer and
        hockey,
    swinging the bat in Tee-ball and baseball,
    jumping in basketball and serving the
        volleyball,
    skating, ice hockey, relay races,
wherever I turn there is a sport to play
and people to play with me.

It takes practice—teamwork and cooperation.
But, what fun!

Except
    when I am picked last for
        the team,
    when the coach yells at me,
    when friends laugh at my
        mistakes.

Help me, God of Playgrounds
    and Fields,
    to be fair and kind,
    to cooperate and to have fun
        being on a team.

First Day of School

A school year begins!

New people to meet,
exciting new things to learn,
new discoveries about the goodness of
your world
and your people, God.

But, I am a little afraid.
Maybe others are, too, even my teachers.

God of New Beginnings,
I know you are with me.

I hear you say my name: "_____,
go forth with my Wisdom and Spirit
to learn and grow."

Thank you. I will.

Going to School

Friend Jesus,
this sure is a cold morning.
    It is so still and quiet.

I like gloves and hats and scarves that
    keep me warm.
But I don't like boots that are too big.
    Mom said I'd grow into them.

Oh, there's my good friend. Do you know her?
I guess you know everybody, Jesus.

Gotta go. School bus is here.
    I'll talk to you later.

Lunchtime

Finally, it's lunch! God, thank you for this food.

Thanks, ____, for making my favorite lunch for me
    and for a friend to share it with.

School

Things aren't going so good, God.

It feels like everybody is smarter than me.
I'm afraid to answer in class.
>I might say something silly and then
>everyone would laugh.

I need courage.

And now homework. Ugh! If I did it
>that might help my school work.
>But I keep forgetting.

And when I finally sit down,
>I find other things to do.

I need help. I think I'll ask _____ to help me.

Playground

Hello, God, this is me.
>I'm at the playground.

So much noise all around me.
>So many people playing.

Just checking in.
>With you, I can be myself.

I want to know you as much as you know me.

New Day

In the morning before I put on my shoes,
I look out my window and say,

> "Good morning, God,
> I'm glad it's a new day.
> Be with me in all I do."

Giving Thanks

God of Thanks, I am thankful
for my parents because _____,
for my family because _____,
for my friends because _____,
for my country because _____,
for my faith because _____,
for your gift, God, of _____.

I will show my gratitude by _____.

God of Thanks, thank you.

My World

Watch the changing clouds,
feel the warm sun,
    the wet rain,
    the fresh snow.

Look at the bright stars in the dark night.

In my world there are
    lively streams,
    roaring oceans,
    tall mighty mountains,
    long sandy beaches,
    trees in all shapes and sizes,
    lacy wild plant life,
    flower fields and grassy meadows.

In my world there are ____.

My world is really YOUR world, God,
    a world for all people.

My world is an OUR world.

Laughter

God of Laughter,
    here I am.
    Can you hear me laughing?

Someone said the funniest thing
    and that silly tingly feeling came inside,
    and I started laughing and couldn't stop.
    My face blushed red
    and laughing tears fell from my eyes.

Laughing with others is fun.
    It is so different from laughing AT someone.
    WITH makes you feel close.
    AT makes you distant.
    Do you know what I mean, God?

One funny thing happened ____.
    I think I told you that already.
    But stories told over and over
    about funny things make me laugh again.

Do you like things that are funny, God?
    When do you laugh?
    Do you have a laughing place?

Senses

My nose can smell ____.
My ears can hear ____.
My eyes can see ____.
My hands can touch ____.
My tongue can taste ____.

Thank you. Thank you. Thank you.

God of Morning

Friend Jesus,
    in my work and in my play,
    be with me through the day.

God of Night

As I lay me down to sleep,
I pray you, God, this child to keep.
Your love guard me through the night
and wake me with the morning light.

I'm Sorry

It sure is hard to say I'm sorry.

First I said it wasn't my fault,
    and it really was a little bit.

I got angry and said mean words.

I need to practice "I'm sorry" a little more
    and try to use kind words. I need to learn
    and hear the sound of an apology.

Help me to begin right now:
    I am sorry for ____.

Now be with me, God of Kindness,
    as I say this to ____.

Storms at Night

The blowing wind whirls and howls. Scary.
The wild wind patters and splatters
    against the window pane. Eerie!

Once asleep, I am now wide awake.
    What should I do?

I am afraid. In the dark, I do not like
    a noisy house.

_____ loves storms—the dancing and singing
    of wind and rain.
I love them, too—DAYTIME storms.

You know, maybe, even in the storms of night,
God of all Whirling Wind and Splattering Rain,
    you dance.

Slow Down

Sit still.
    Slowly breathe in and breathe out.
    Become aware of God's presence.

Talk with God.
    Listen.
    Thank God for being in your life.

My Body

Wonderful God,
   thank you for my body.

Bodies come in all shapes and sizes—
   fat, thin, tall, short
   and different ones IN-BETWEEN.

Right now, I'm IN-BETWEEN.

But whatever size or shape,
   you love all bodies just the same, God.

I thank you, God,
   because I am so wonderfully made.
   Wonderful are your works.

Quiet Prayer

God lives in me.

   Place your hand on your heart.
   Pretend that you are alone with God.

Hear God call your name: "_____, I love you."

   Rest in God's presence and love.

If you start thinking about other things, say:

   "I love you, God."

Sit still and give God your love.

Jealousy

Sometimes I look at the clothes or shoes
  someone is wearing
  and I am jealous. I WANT what they have!

And then sometimes, I look and say,
  "I'm glad I don't wear clothes or shoes
  like THAT!"

Help me to remember that it is not
  how I look on the OUTSIDE that counts,
  but what I am on the INSIDE.

INSIDE we are all the same
  with feelings, a heart, mind and spirit.

And you, God, you live INSIDE each one of us.

Word Prayer

Choose one line to say today:
  "Loving God, I am here." OR
  "Jesus, I love you, help me today." OR
  "Speak God, I am listening."

In your busy day, listen to your words,
  say them often,
  take them into your heart
  and walk them in your feet all day.

Hugging Prayer

Try to remember a time when you were
    at the beach.

Pretend you are sitting on that beach.
    Is it hot?
    Is there a breeze blowing?
    What do you see?
    What sounds do you hear?
    What do you smell?

Stretch out your hands.
    What do they feel?
    Are you alone?
    Are you with others?
    How do you feel inside?

See Jesus walk across the sand and sit with you.
    Tell him what is happening in your life.
    Then, listen to him.

It is time to go.
    Say good-bye.
    Give Jesus a hug.
    Feel Jesus hugging you.
    Promise you will meet again.

Object Prayer

I walked the beach a long time
    before I found this shell.
Someone told me it was once
    a house for a hermit crab.
God, you are like this house.
    In you, I feel safe.

My bare branch has tiny buds.
    There is even a speck of green.
There must be life inside.
    God, you are like this tiny bud inside of me.
    Help me to grow.

A rock. Strong. Rain, storms, floods,
    and still you are here.
Be my rock, God. There is so much change in
    my family right now.
I am afraid. I need your strength.

Choose one of these objects:
   What does it say to you about God?
   What does it say about you?

Wind and Spirit

Hush. Stand still. Listen. Is this
    the wind sound for a clear day,
    the wind sound for rain,
    the wind sound for a heavy storm?

Hush. Stand still. Be quiet. Is this
    the Spirit voice of peace,
    the Spirit voice of joy,
    the Spirit voice of hope?

Whisper again. I am listening,
    God of Wind and Spirit.

Gift Prayer

"What you are is God's gift to you.
    What you become is your gift to God."

Be quiet. Read the words above again.
    Tell God how you feel about these words.

Decide:
    My gift is ____.
    I will share it by ____.
    Thank you, God, for being in my life.

Breath Prayer

Place your feet on the floor.
Open your hands on your lap.
Sit straight as if a string is pulling you upright.

Become aware of your feet and relax them.
Relax your hands, shoulders, face. Say:

I want to have a listening body, God.

Notice your breathing. Don't change it.
Just be aware of it. Pretend that you are breathing in God's love.

As you breathe out, send that love to someone you care about.

Breathe in. Breathe out.

Whisper Prayer

Fold your hands together.
  Whisper a prayer in them.

Pretend that prayer is going
  all through your body.

Stand and bow
  with hands in prayer
  to the God in everyone.

PART TWO

Prayers for Others

"Love one another."
John 15:12

For Parents and Stepparents

God of Mothers and Fathers,
    protect our parents and stepparents
    with your kindness.

Make them strong when they are tired.
Comfort them when they are worried.
Encourage them when they are overwhelmed.
Surround them with peace and hope
    when they are afraid.

Give them thankful hearts when things go well,
    and in hard times, loving kindness.

I love them today, tomorrow and forever.

For Grandparents

Thank you, God, for Grandma ____
    and the way she ____.

Thank you, God, for Grandpa ____
    and the way he ____.

They are special to me.
    Thank you that I am special to them, too.

Please, God, take care of them.

For Brothers and Sisters

I like my brother(s) and sister(s).

We play together and laugh a lot—
    sometimes at silly things.

Often, they are pests, I mean PESTS,
    using my things without asking,
    arguing,
    wanting their way,
    and when cleanup time comes,
        I'm the only one around.

But when I'm sad or down,
    they cheer me up;
    they listen to me
        when things go wrong at school.

When I try something difficult,
    they cheer me on.

I like having my brother(s) _____
    and my sister(s) _____
    because we can _____ together.

God of Brothers and Sisters, thank you.

For Those Who Are Sick

Healer God,
　　let your Spirit watch over those who are
　　sick, especially ____.

Help those who care for the sick everywhere:
　　relatives, doctors, nurses, friends.
　　Give them a healing touch.

Picture in your mind the person for whom
　　you are praying.

Send your love and care to this person. Say:

　　May our voices bring comfort to the sick.
　　May our hands give loving care.

For Others at Night

Please God, help ____ to get well.

Help people in troubled lands
   make peace with each other.

I am so tired of fighting with ____.
   Help me to get along better with ____.

Take care of ____, who seems so worried.
   And help ____.

God, take care of yourself.
   If anything happens to you,
   we're in big trouble.

For Teachers

Spirit of Truth,
    bless my teachers.

Guide them in thought, word and deed.
    Let them be signs of your patience
    and love, God, as I learn and grow.

For All Who Help

In your goodness, God,
> bless all these people in my family: ____ .

And bless all those good and loving people
who help me:
> teachers who guide,
> babysitters who care,
> police and firefighters who protect,
> doctors and nurses who heal,
> farmers who grow food,
> those who sweep, clean and pick up trash,
> and for ____ .

Thank you for all who help.

Pebble Prayer

*Find a small bag and a handful of pebbles.
Give a person's name to each pebble. Say:*

> With this pebble, I think about ____ ,
> and I pray that God gives this person
> what he or she needs today.

*As you pray for each person, put a pebble in
your prayer bag. Carry the prayer bag in your
pocket or place it in your room. Let it remind
you of all the needs of others.*

For Pets

Thank you, God, for our pets,
  for the huggy friendship of our dogs,
  for the purr of our cats,
  for the mischief of our hamsters,
  for the quiet of our fish,
  for the song sounds of our birds,
  and especially for our pet ____.

I have so much fun with my pet.

For Sick Pets

My pet, ____, is sick and I am sad.

Bless my pet.
  Give ____ strength to get better.

My pet can't tell me what he or she is feeling,
  but let me show my pet I care.

For Someone Who Has Died

God, Creator of All,
    I feel very sad. ____ has died.
    It hurts so much to lose someone I love.

I know I cannot understand all your ways.
    I know you have reasons for everything,
        even dying,
    but I don't know what to think
        when people die.

I know they go to live with you forever,
    but I am still sad and miss them a lot.

Help me to understand my sadness
    and the sadness of others, God.

For People Hurting

Violence. War. Crime.
    Tornadoes. Hurricanes. Floods.

On our television I saw pictures of ____.
    Some children are hungry.
    Some people have no place to live.
    Some grownups can't find jobs.

God, be their strength. Help them.

For the Handicapped

Bless and help those
    who are crippled and cannot walk
        or play running and jumping games,

    who are blind and cannot see trees, flowers
        and the faces of family and friends,

    who are deaf and cannot hear birds
        and rain, music and voices,

    and give strength to those who find it
        hard to keep up with class work,
        reading and writing and numbers.

Help me, God, to help them in the right way
    so we can all grow together.

We need each other.

For the Homeless

God of Homes and Shelters,
    please give shelter to all the people
    in the world who have
        no real home to live in,
        no place to go when it rains and storms,
        no house to rest in when they are tired.

Ease their cares.

God, I know you help others
    through kids like me.

Maybe I could give some of my allowance
    to shelters that offer beds and food.

Thank you for the hands that built my house
    and for the bed where I sleep
    and the table where I eat.

Please, let my hands take care of the homeless
    everywhere.

A Room Blessing

Bless this room, God.
> May this be a place of peace and laughter.

Give shelter to those who rest here.
> Be with them in all that they do.

A Doorway Blessing

Peace to this house
> and to all who dwell in it.

Peace to them that enter
> and to them that depart.

A Home Blessing

God of Homes,
> we are one. We are your people.

Bless our homes with your presence.
Bless our hearts with your love.
Bless our hopes and dreams and joys.
Bless our family with good health.
Bless each room of our home.
Bless all places where we live.

> *Bless your home with water.*

For Our World Family

Today, God, we remember our world family:
  for boys and girls in school,
  for men and women at work,
  for the lonely, the sick, the homeless.

May each person have a happy moment,
  a special moment with a friend,
  a quiet moment to think,
  a peace-filled time to play.

May God bless all our brothers and sisters
  in the world today.

Sign of the Cross

In the name of the Father,
and of the Son,
and of the Holy Spirit. Amen.

Our Father

Our Father,
   who art in heaven,
   hallowed be your name,
   your kingdom come,
   your will be done on earth as it is in heaven.

Give us this day our daily bread
   and forgive us our trespasses
   as we forgive those who trespass against us,

and lead us not into temptation,
   but deliver us from evil.
         Amen.

Hail Mary

Hail, Mary,
   full of grace,
   the Lord is with you.

Blessed are you among women,
   and blessed is the fruit
   of your womb, Jesus.

Holy Mary, mother of God,
   pray for us sinners,
   now and at the hour of our death.
   Amen.

Glory Be

Glory be to the Father,
and to the Son,
and to the Holy Spirit,

as it was in the beginning,

is now,

and will be forever.

Amen.

PART THREE

Prayers for the Week

"You are my people."
Colossians 3:12

Sunday
Family Prayer of Promise

Friend Jesus,
    we _____ accept family life.

We promise to be with one another
    in good and bad times.

We promise to be faithful.
We promise to love and forgive.
We promise to be patient.

We promise to welcome you as a friend
    into our family life.

We promise to honor one another
    all the days of our life.

In the name of the Father, the Son and
    the Holy Spirit.

    Amen.

Monday
Family Prayer of Peace

Friend Jesus,
    may we be makers of peace.

May we walk in peace.
May we work in peace.
May we live in peace.
May we be at peace with ourselves and others.

Ask your family to pray with you the peace
    pledge below.
Place your hand over your heart.
Stand and say together the peace pledge.

We pledge ourselves to peace everywhere.
We promise to care for earth and sea and air,
    to respect and love all living things,
    and to say thank you
    for the gifts God brings.

Tuesday
Family Prayer of Praise

For sunlight, shade,
    GLORY BE. WE PRAISE YOU, GOD.

For stones, rocks, pebbles, mud and earth,
    GLORY BE. WE PRAISE YOU, GOD.

For willow trees, climbing vines, leaves,
    fields of clover,
    GLORY BE. WE PRAISE YOU, GOD.

For tiny insects, ladybugs, grasshoppers,
    GLORY BE. WE PRAISE YOU, GOD.

For rushing water, still pools, waterfalls,
    GLORY BE. WE PRAISE YOU, GOD.

For boys and girls, women and men,
    fathers and mothers,
    aunts and uncles, sisters and brothers,
    GLORY BE. WE PRAISE YOU, GOD.

Glory be to all that you have made.

How wonderful you are God!
We will always shout your praises!

Wednesday
Family Prayer of Ears, Eyes and Heart

God of Blessings,

Bless our eyes so that we can see
    your presence in others,
    in your creation, in your world.

    Make the Sign of the Cross on your eyes.

Bless our ears so that we can hear your word,
    your message, your Good News.

    Make the Sign of the Cross on your ears.

Bless our hearts so that we can understand
    your presence in all that we do.

    Make the Sign of the Cross on your heart.

Thursday
Family Prayer of Faith

As a sign of faith, stand for this creed.

We celebrate you, God,
    because we believe in you.

We believe in you as Creator
    who made this wonderful world.

We believe in you as Jesus
    who became like us
    so that we could become like him.

We believe in you as Spirit
    who keeps this world going
    through so much love.

We believe life is so important
    it will go on forever.

We believe in plants, animals,
    birds and flowers.

We believe in all the people
    that have been made,
    that together with you, God,
    we can laugh and love forever.

Amen.

Friday
Family Prayer of Love

God of Love,
sometimes we fail to love.
> We talk about our friends.
> We turn away from those in need.
> We become angry.
> We act without thinking first.
> We forget to say, "I love you."

Help us to love you, God,
> with our whole heart,
> our whole mind,
> our whole soul,
> and to love our neighbors as ourselves.

Saturday
Family Prayer of Glory Be

Glory Be to God!

Peace to God's people.

Beauty to all creation—
    to the seasons,
    to the animals,
    to flowers, trees, pineapples and butterflies,
    to boys and girls, men and women,
    to all that God has made.

Goodness to my family _____.

Glory Be. Glory Be. Glory Be.

Meal Family Prayer

God of all Creation,
    bless this meal
    and bless the people who share this meal.

We thank you, God, for important things:
    for health,
    for food,
    for shelter,
    for life,
    for forgiveness,
    for people who love and care,
    for ____.

Blessed are you, God of all Creation.

Through this goodness we have this bread to share.

Break bread and give a piece to each family member.

Morning Family Prayer

God of the Morning,
　　bless us this day with your nearness.

Help us to show love to our family,
　　to be kind to our friends,
　　to be helpful to the people we meet.

With you, God, we will grow.
　　Thank you for all the day's goodness.

We bow our heads for the blessing of the day:
　　May God bless you and keep you.
　　May God look kindly on you.
　　May God give you peace.

Evening Family Prayer

God of the Evening,
> thank you for this good world.
> Thank you for the life of this day.

Take care of my family and friends, ____.
> I love them.
> I thank them for loving me.
> I love you, too, friend Jesus.

Be with me as I sleep and make me ready
> to meet tomorrow with a smile.

Ask your parent or other family member to make the Sign of the Cross on your forehead and say the words below:

Thank you for this child, Gracious God.
> ____ is a precious gift.

Autumn Family Prayer

Hold your hands open.

God of Autumn,

For the fall colors,
    we thank you, God.

For the food of the harvest,
    we thank you, God.

For the smells and sounds of the season,
    we thank you, God.

Hold hands open and higher.

Our good earth,
    we give to you, God.

Our family and friends,
    we give to you, God.

Our hopes and dreams,
    we give to you, God.

Winter Family Prayer

Winter God,
In peace,
    we bless you for dark long nights to rest,
    for the excitement of blustery storms,
    sleet, ice and snowy skies.

In peace,
    we bless you for the warmth of
    wood-burning stoves,
    fireplaces, heat from radiators,
    for blankets, afghans, quilts and sweaters.

In peace,
    we bless the four directions of our winter world:
    To the north, may you live in peace.
    To the east, may you live in peace.
    To the south, may you live in peace.
    To the west, may you live in peace.

Wherever we turn,
    we see the face of God.

In peace bless each family member.

Spring Family Prayer

God of Spring,
    rivers flow.
    Fruit trees flower.
    Seeds sprout green.

Make us aware of the season of Spring.

Give us feet to walk humbly
    and hands to touch gently
    this garden earth,
    Springtime God.

Summer Family Prayer

Spirit of God,
    leaves rustle.
    Kites fly.
    Trees bend.
    Grasses dance.
    Hair blows across my face.

We are alive with God's breath, the wind.

Spirit of God, move through our prayers
    and take them to your people of north,
    south, east and west.

PART FOUR

Prayers for Special Times

"Let us be happy and celebrate."
Psalm 117:24

Birthday

God of Birthdays,
    we light this candle in honor of ____
    who has been your light and gift to others.

Bless ____.

Open ____'s eyes to see the beauty
    and wonder of our world.

Give ____ courage to face difficulties and
    strength to handle them.

Bless ____ with health and happiness.

God of Birthdays,
    thank you for parents who gave ____ life,
    for sisters, brothers, grandparents, relatives,
    who nourish that life.

May we come together for many years as family
    to celebrate this day of birth.

Sing "Happy Birthday."
Kiss the birthday person and say "I love you."

Labor Day

As family, we make our pledge of work.

We promise to work hard,
to make a new world and
to thank people
for the work they do

in your name, God, Maker of All Creation.

St. Francis' Day (October 4)

I celebrate sun, moon
and stars, wind and air,
water, fire and earth!

I call them my brothers
and sisters
as Francis did
in living a life of praise
to you,
God of All Praise.

Halloween (October 31)

God, protect me on this night
    as I walk the streets of my neighborhood.

Help me to treat others kindly
    and not trick them by what I do or say.

I know your spirit is with me.

Thanksgiving Day

God of all Gratitude,
    this is a day of thanksgiving!

We say, THANK YOU, GOD,
    for all gifts, great and small,
    for water, wind, fire and earth,
    THANK YOU, GOD;

    for beginnings, middles and ends,
    and all the moments of living
    and working together,
    THANK YOU, GOD;

    for smiles, hopes, dreams
    and being able to say kind words to others,
    THANK YOU, GOD;
    for mothers, fathers, sisters, brothers,

grandparents, aunts, uncles and cousins,
THANK YOU, GOD;

for all that you have made,
THANK YOU, GOD.

God looked at everything that had been made
and was very pleased.
We are, too.

Thank you. Thank you. Thank you.

*Stand in silent thanksgiving for a few moments,
thanking God for the gift of each person in
the family.*

Advent

Come every day into my heart, Jesus.
   I want to prepare for your
   special coming at Christmas.

Help me to get ready inside to welcome you
   and to celebrate your birthday.

Come, friend Jesus, come!

Christmas (December 25)

God of Gifts,
   you love us so much that you send
   your son as a gift to us.

Jesus is the light of the world, our light.

Praise to you, God.
   Glory for the birthday of Jesus!

Place the figure of the infant Jesus in your
nativity scene manger and sing "Silent Night."

New Year (January 1)

God of New Beginnings,
    with the hope of a new world,
    bless this year.

With the promise of new life,
    bless this year.

With the dream of a better tomorrow,
    bless this year.

God, give us the joy of New Beginnings.
    Bless this year and be with us
    as we work to make this old world
    into a new one.

*Toast the new year or salute it in your own
family's tradition.*

Epiphany
(January 6)

Thank you, God,
for giving Jesus
to all of us.

As the light of the star
showed Jesus,
so let us
become a light
that shows Jesus
to others.

Arise and shine out,
our light has come.
The glory of God shines upon us.
Shout the praises of God.

Valentine's Day (February 14)

God of Love,
   on Valentine's Day,

I thank you for people
   who show me how to love
   by the way they live their lives.

Bless me with patient and kind love.

Bless me with love that forgives
   and forgets the wrongs of others.

Bless me with generous and courteous love.

Bless these people that I love: ____.

Mardi Gras
(Shrove Tuesday or
Fat Tuesday)

God of Celebrations,
    many different countries have a party today.

There is food and music,
    laughter and dancing.
      It is fun to have a good time, God.

Tomorrow we begin our journey through Lent,
    but today, **HOORAY!**

Ash Wednesday

Friend Jesus,
    your ashes are marked upon me.

Your cross reminds me to be open
    to new experiences, even hard ones.

During Lent, I will take up your cross,
    and mine, and follow you.

Lent

Friend Jesus, Lent is a journey with you.
>Forty days can be a long time.
>Am I praying?
>Am I listening to others?
>Am I helping others?
>Am I walking with you?

St. Patrick's Day (March 17)

May the road rise up to meet you.
May the wind be always at your back.
May the sun shine warm upon your face
>and the rains fall soft upon your fields.

And until we meet again,
>may you be held
>in the palm
>of God's hand.

I love this Irish blessing!

St. Joseph's Day (March 19)

Like Joseph, I like to work hard, God,
    and to finish what I begin.

A job well done gives me a good feeling.
    Be with me as I do my work.

Easter

Alleluia! Alleluia! Hooray!
   You have risen as
   you said, Jesus.

I, too, will rise one day.
   This is a day for
   rejoicing!

A Day for Mary

Like Mary,
>   let me say yes to your being
>   in my life, friend Jesus.

Like Mary,
>   let me live for others.

Pentecost

I am an Alleluia!

I am a Wonder!

The gifts of your Spirit, God, make me so.
>   With these gifts, I can live your life, Jesus.

I can be fully alive!

Mother's Day

I love you, Mom. I love your aliveness,
    your joy in living, your understanding,
    your giving.

And what I love best of all
    is that you love me.

God of all Mothers,
    thank you for my mom!

Father's Day

Thank you, friend Jesus,
    for my father who loves me,
    for my grandfather who cares for me,
    and for God, your father and mine,
    who made me and is always with me.

How lucky I am!

Independence Day (July 4)

God of Freedom,
    you made us free—free to love you,
    ourselves and others. What a gift!

I celebrate today the rights of all people
    to life, liberty and the pursuit of happiness.
    Throughout the earth, let freedom ring.

Ring bells or sing songs that celebrate America.